Ricochet'
and Other FUN Games with an Odd Ball

by Chris Cavert

a **FUN**doing publication

Published in conjunction with
Learning Unlimited Corporation
1-888-622-4203

D1158842

What are people saying?

*"Toss the Ricochet' ball high in the air,
watch it come down, then bounce everywhere.
You move and try to catch it,
Catch it if you can.
These games are made for every child, woman and man."*
W. Clay Fiske, III, Poet, Adventurer & Challenge Program Director

*"Ricochet' is like life; sometimes the ball is in hand,
sometimes it's in your crotch, but you're still playing!"*
Karl Rohnke, Gamesman and Author of over 10 experiential adventure activity books.

"When I travel and play with people around the world, the R-Ball is always with me. The reaction (no pun intended) to this novel piece of recreational equipment is truly unbelievable. It's great for a variety of games and it is a wonderful coordination tool as well. I recommend the R-Ball, and these Odd Ball games, to anyone looking for a unique way to program for today's playful youth."
Mike Spiller, Owner - Games of the World

"There is no 'I' in Ricochet'!"
Brian Brolin, Adventure Program Director & International Trainer

"As ons hier ricochet' speel, en ek hoor iemand se "kan ek saam speel", besef ek weer eens dat dit is waar die wonder van Ricochet' begin."
(When we play Ricochet' here in South Africa and I hear someone say "can we play with" - I realize that's where the wonder (magic) of Ricochet' starts.)
Anne-Marie Kruger, International gamer

"I am always on the lookout for fun, easily adaptable, low-prop games that teach and Ricochet' is an original game that manages to be all three. I love the fact that I can adapt this game for so many different populations. Ricochet' can be competitive or non-competitive, easy or nearly impossible, appropriate for kids or adults and yet no matter how you adapt it, it is always fun and . . . it fits into your pocket! No 'bag-of-tricks' is complete without a Ricochet' ball."
Denise Pratt, Experiential Educator, Educational Trainer and World Traveler

"Para todos los jovenes de corazon. Todos los que no han perdido el sentido de aventura . . . porque nunca sabes donde va a caer esta "pelotita" Ricochet."
(For all the young at heart. All those that have not lost their sense of wonder . . . because you never know where that little Ricochet' ball is going to go next!)
Susana Acosta, All around incredible person & Official Spanish Translator for Ricochet' International.

"I have been using the Ricochet' ball in corporate team building for several years. It's a great prop to have when a team needs an activity to practice focus, goal setting, and communication."
Sam Sikes, Vice President - Learning Unlimited Corporation

"I'm always searching for new, fun places to play these games. They are very engaging and loads of FUN. A definite must have for your bag or tricks."
Michelle Cummings, Owner - Training Wheels and First Class Entrepreneur

"So, you play with chew toys, eh?" **Paul**
"Yeah, and I can't stop!" **Chris**

"English, Afrikaans, Sotho, Tswana, Spanish, Swahili, German . . .the games play well in all languages. These just happen to be the ones I've played in."
Brian Brolin, Odd Ball games enthusiast

"In just 15 minutes I was convinced. Finally, some activities that are perfect for hard surfaces. Tennis courts, basketball courts, playgrounds and driveways will never be the same again."
Jim Cain, Ph.D., Author - Teamwork and Teamplay

"Ricochet' is a game that takes kids that are told the "can't', kids that say, 'I won't' and kids that just don't, and make them say, 'Let's do it again!'"
Brian Brolin, Educator

"Whether they are a 7 year old kid or a 50 year old corporate executive, the R-Ball has been a powerful tool in facilitating change. It's hard to imagine how such a fun activity can have so many take-aways."
Steve Fleming, Co-owner of Group Dynamix

"I've played Ricochet' with my sister, my neighbor, my co-workers, my fiancée, my friends, my nephews, and my cat. I had a blast every time. Except with the cat, who had a little trouble serving."
Brian Brolin, Can't get enough of Ricochet' and a good friend of Chris'

Ricochet'

and Other FUN Games
with an Odd Ball
by Chris Cavert

Thanks

I have been really blessed to have great friends and Ricochet' partners along the way. My first thanks go out to the pioneer Ricochet' players, J. B. and E. P. (I'm protecting their identities just in case!)

More thanks go to Mike Spiller and Karl Rohnke for their great ideas and their energy for the game. A special thanks to my copy editors, Susana and Denise; to Sam, without your help this book would still be on my hard drive; and to my friend David Smith for all the great pictures! Finally, thank you to all the Ricochet' players along the way, the record holders, the innovators, and those crazy people who play Ricochet' on ice, we are bonded for life. May you live long and PLAY EVERY DAY!

<u>And a word to the wise</u>

Catch it, if you can!

Please keep safety your number one concern whenever setting up and playing any of these games. Watch out for Span danger's edges, loose gravel, poles, fences, player gear... ball in the nose... and the like. Please remember, the intention here is FUN by all means! So, have at it my friends!

Contents

Intro

Welcome to the fast action of the Ricochet' experience! The games presented in this book are intended to bring players together in a new arena of discovery and adventure. Some games are competitive, others are cooperative, but all are presented in the spirit of "Coopetition". I challenge you and your coopetitioners to play the games within an environment of safety both physical & mental. Always take care of yourself & others before all else. Without players there would be no games.

The format of the activities is used to give specific information to those who find it useful. However, please keep your mind open to adaptations as you see fit.

Format includes:

Application: This will give the reader the intended use of the game and what sort of Span (playing surface) the game requires, as well as some limitations.

Needs: What you will need for the game including additional Span info.

Number of Players: Based on best action-to-play ratio.

Suggested Age: This is based on the play of the game versus reflex development (findings based on feedback from a variety of sources).

Play: The basic directions of the game.

Scenario: This section is used where a play-by-play description might help the reader better visualize the game.

Note: Any other information that might be important or FYI.

Ideas, Records & Places: The space provided is for additional considerations the reader would like to add or for record keeping on game scores, memorable moments and places played.

PLEASE, always use caution when playing any of the games presented here. As it was once quoted during a Ricochet' session, This ain't a toy man! (Well it really is a toy, but you get the meaning!?)

Be careful, watch out, and have fun that's what its all about!

Body, Mind, Spirit & Experiential Educators

If you are an educator you might be interested in some of the educational benefits these Odd Ball games might produce. I will assume that as soon as I put these educational advancements on paper more will surely arise. So please keep in mind the overwhelming possibilities of Odd Ball adventures in the learning movement of our new Millennium – go to www.fundoing.com for the latest Odd Ball developments.

Body Many movement and body skills can be enhanced through the use of these Odd Ball games. Among the many skill that can be learned from these games, participants will increase their Bilateral abilities (using both sides of the body for catching and moving), Eye-Hand and Eye-Foot coordination (moving the body based on the needs of the activity), Tracking (following a moving object through space), Focus (being able to maintain attention to a task and action) and Peripheral Awareness (being able to see and be aware of what is happening around you as you are focusing on a task or action). Many of the games will also involve some aerobic movements that will strengthen the heart and couldn't we use stronger hearts today!

Mind What can the Mind gain? Players will use auditory memory - learning specific vocabulary and apply the words to the appropriate situations. Visual discrimination will be used to determine what is the ball and what is not. Different attentions are used as well in many of the games visual, auditory, motor and spatial needs. The mind can then determine which attention is best in different actions and events. Memory recall is also very important, especially if you are keeping score. I've also been told that a science teacher has used the game, bReak out to teach the scientific method – cool! The sky is the limit (In some games it might be the ceiling!)

3

Spirit The spirit I like to teach with these games is the spirit of fun and play. Under this roof includes teaching Coopetition (competing cooperatively to make the game worth playing for everyone), and adventuresomeness (choosing to take chances and play the game to the limits within the safe environment of the group). If we can play, learn, and grow in a safe place how will this influence our attitudes, behaviors, tolerance and our interactions with others? How will this safe place touch our spirit? It is up to all of us to make it fun and make it last!

Experiential Educators I know there are those of you out there (including myself) who like to process and reflect on activities to enhance learning and the transfer of learning. Due to the intended purpose of this book I decided not add the experiential information to the activities. However, if you would like more information in addition to what you will come up with, go to my web site at: www.fundoing.com - once there, click on the Ricochet' link. On this page you will find processing and reflection considerations for most of the activities and ways to frontload some of them to focus on different considerations. This page will also include additional activities that have been shared with me by colleagues and friends, world record scores, and historical pictures. And, don't forget to keep in touch and share your discoveries as well!

Enjoy!
Chris Cavert

The History of Ricochet' And Thus Other FUN Games With An Odd Ball

As in everything (well, I would think everything) there is a history - some histories are more interesting than others are, but nonetheless a history. The game of Ricochet' is no exception. Here's the story as it is true for me. In the early spring of 1992, I was doing some shopping at one of my favorite everything's-a-dollar stores in Saint Joseph, Missouri. At the time (and come to think of it, still the time) I bought all my spherical objects (balls of different types) in denominations of three – I was into juggling back then as well. I was wandering through the "Dog Toy" section of the store when I stumbled across my first three (what are now known as) Ricochet' Balls. (I don't remember the original name on the packaging.) As always, I was happy to find an interesting tossable object and put it in my basket to add to my collection of tossables. Little did I know at the time what the future would hold for this Odd ball!

Some time had passed before I dragged a couple of friends out to the sidewalk of our residence in Atchison, Kansas to see what this interesting ball would do. (This sidewalk would become one of our favorite Spans to play on.)

We began by just tossing the ball into the air and chasing it around for a while. It reminded us of Popcorn bopping around on a hot surface. So there it was – Popcorn. This was the original name of Ricochet'. As we played Popcorn we started to name some of the actions the ball was taking. One action became a Ricochet' – a ball that angled drastically away from the Receiver. This action seemed to personify the game as a whole and the word instilled a bit more curiosity to potential players. What catches your interest better, "Hey, let's go play some Popcorn!" or, "Hey, let's go play some 'Ricochet'!" (This one rhymes too!) – see what I mean. And there you have it, the history of the

5

game that's sweeping the nation (pretty soon!).

So, for all you trivia buffs out there (can you remember without peeking?) – "What was the original name of the game Ricochet'?" "Where was the first game played?" "How many players played the first game?" (If you get this one without looking, you're good!) "What is a Span?" (If you figured this one out without looking, you're really good!) If you didn't get that one, read on my friends and enjoy!!

Ricochet' Lingo

All right! Are you Ready!!? First things first. If you want to be a top notch Ricochet' (or, "R-ball" if you're "into" the game) player, you've got to get the lingo. Impress your friends and opponents as you voice your varied verbiage on the Span. What's a Span? Read on and be enlightened!!

Action-Time – The time during a game when the Ricochet' ball is moving and being counted for Points.

Back-Lash – When the Ricochet' ball angles drastically back towards the Receiver after the first bounce. (My friend Karl likes to call this one the "Cup Carom" [non-specific gender]. You'll pick up more on this idea as you play the games.)

Catch – When the Ricochet' ball comes to rest in a Receiver's hand(s). The ball must be deemed in control by a majority of players in the game for the Receiver to get the counted number of Points (if playing a catch-for-Points game).

Closing Score – The number of Points, agreed upon by all players, for winning a game, i.e., play to 10 win by 2.

(Coopetition) – Even though there are some games that are competitive in nature, it will take the cooperation of all players to play the games and keep them safe.

Count – A Receiving player can call a, "Count" if he or she feels that a Done-Ball call was made in haste. There must be a majority agreement by all the Non-Receiving players to either keep the call or reverse it. In some cases a Re-Throw is made.

Done-Ball – A ball that is no longer playable. See also, Dud, Roller/Dibble, & Touch.

Down-Time – The time between Action-Times when players can catch their breath, and prepare for the next Throw, Round, or Game.

Dud – When the Ricochet' ball comes to a dead stop after hitting or landing on a soft surface like grass or clothing. In most cases, the counted Points for that Throw are lost, or the Round is over (depending on what game you are playing).

Etiquette Play (EP) – When the players agree, before a game begins, to follow Ricochet' Etiquette Play (see, Etiquette Play section).

Fetch – Retrieving the Ricochet' ball from some (often far away) area after the Action-Time of a Throw has been called a Roller, Dud or Done-Ball.

Field-R – Going after the Ricochet' ball in the front or backfield during the game, oveR the line.

Hand – This is done during Etiquette Play when a player hands (or hands off) the Ricochet' ball to another player. The ball never loses contact with hands during a Hand.

Hinder – If a Non-Receiving player touches the ball during Action -Time or gets in the way, contact is made, of the Receiver. A Re-Throw is given.

Nature of Play – Agreed upon by all players before a game begins. How will players treat each other, what will be expected of all players, etc. I will always encourage Etiquette Play at all times (see, Etiquette Play section).

Non-Receiving Player – All players, other than the Receiver, on the Span during Action-Time. The job of the Non-Receiving Players will be to monitor the safety of the Receiving players, count Points, and judge Done-Balls.

Playing Line – A line used in a game as a boundary or scoring zone indicator.

Point – The time when the Ricochet' ball touches the Span during Action-Time (depending on the game being played).

Push – This is an action during "Doubles" Ricochet' when one team partner pushes the Ricochet' ball back to the ground to extend the length of the Action-Time on the ball. One of the partners can call, "Push" to indicate that they will take the Push so their partner can be ready for the Catch.

Rabbit – When the Ricochet' ball takes off across the Span on a fast paced, hard-to-catch, low trajectory bouncing pattern away from the Receiver. The bounces can still be distinguishable as counted Points. The Rabbit, more often than not, turns into a Roller, or a Dud before it is caught for Points.

R-Ball – The nickname used for Ricochet' if you are really "into" the game. It adds to the "cool" factor of the experience.

Re-Throw – There are some games where it will be allowed to call a Re-Throw. Only the Receiver of a Throw can call a Re-Throw. If the Receiver determines, after the Throw has been made and before the Ricochet' ball touches the Span for the first time, that the throw of the ball will put him or her at a disadvantage, a verbal, "Re-Throw" can be called. If a Re-Throw is called, any player can Fetch the ball and bring it back to the Thrower for another Throw. Example: Let's say on the Throw from the Thrower, the ball's trajectory leads us to believe that it will land away from the center of the group and near the edge of the Span, before it bounces, a, "Re-Throw" can be called.

Receiver/Receiving Team – The player (or team of players) who is (are) up in turn to catch the ball for Points after a Throw is made by a Thrower or Serving Team.

Ricochet' – When the Ricochet' ball angles drastically away from the Receiver after the first bounce on the Span.

Rocket – A Throw as high as overhead space allows. This can be done in an underhand method, tossing the ball as high as possible, or some players may choose the, lean-back-overhand-throw-straight-up-in-the-air method. In either case, you want the Ricochet' ball to come down near the center of the Span that your playing on – this is the challenge of the Rocket.

Roller / Dibble – A Roller

is called, by any player other than the Receiver, when the Ricochet' ball starts to dibble (not a misprint) across the Span. Rollers or Dibbles are indistinguishable bounces – bounces so fast that they cannot be counted with accuracy. The words Roller and Dibble are interchangeable during a game. Once a Roller/Dibble is called, the Action-Time is over for that Receiver and no Points are gained for that Throw. (A Receiver can contest a Roller call by asking for a "Count". If there is less than a majority ruling by the other Non-Receiving Players, that it was in fact a Roller/Dribble, then the Receiver can get another Throw or be rewarded the Points counted if the ball was caught.)

Round – (depending on the game) A Round consists of each player (or team) in the game taking one Throw and Receiving one Throw. A Round can also be considered over

when the ball is determined to be a Done-Ball.

Scoring Zone – The area of the Span behind a Playing Line in oveR the line where, if the Ricochet' ball touches, a Point is awarded to one team.

Serving Team – The

team, as a whole, that tosses or Throws (serves) the Ricochet' ball to an opposing team who then plays the ball for possible Points.

Skyscraper – A Throw in-between a Rocket and a Sneaker.

Sneaker – The lowest Throw allowed. The Ricochet' ball must be Thrown at a height that, at least, exceeds the height of the tallest player in the group.

Span – The Span is the playing surface for any game played with a Ricochet' ball. Spans that have been used: Sidewalks, Tennis Courts, Streets, Basketball Courts, Racquetball Courts, Volleyball Courts, Cement Slabs, Carpeted Slabs, Pool Decks, Table Tops, Wood Platforms, and one of my favorites, a Sheet of Ice!?

Throw – When the Ricochet' ball leaves the hand of a player, most often in an underhand method, and moves directly up away from the Thrower.

Thrower – A Non-Receiving Player who makes a Throw.

Toe-The-Line – Players must have both big toes on the Playing Line of the game – yes, you can keep your shoes on.

Toss – When the Ricochet' ball leaves the hand of a player, underhand or overhand, and moves somewhat parallel to the Span. The specific intent of the Toss is to get the ball to another player during Down-Time. THE TOSS IS NEVER ACCEPTABLE DURING ETIQUETTE PLAY (see, Etiquette Play section). When Etiquette Play is in progress and a player Tosses the ball, it is customary to point your finger at the Tossing player and call this player a, "Tosser" (just one time is enough, no need to repeat the call!!). Why don't we like to toss? If a player drops a Toss you spend more Down-Time Fetching the ball.

Tosser – The name given to a player who Tosses the ball to another player during Etiquette Play Down-Time.

Touch - Any time a ball hits or touches a player during Action-Time and then contacts the ground. In most games a Done-Ball is called after a Touch. During some variations, usually during games where you're just learning, Touches may be allowed and Action-Time can continue.

WALL! – This call is made (usually in a very loud voice, or voices), to warn a player of impending contact with an immovable object – like a wall, fence, tree, or pole. The Action-Time can continue if the ball hits a wall, if of course, the Points can continue to be counted. However, Points may or may not be counted off the Walls. It depends on what you set up during the initial Nature of Play. (If you play in a Racquetball Court you may choose to count Points off the walls.)

Lingo words are capitalized within the text so you can reference them if you need to. Have Fun!

✳ ———————————————————————— ✳

Etiquette Play

My intention with all of these games is to create an atmosphere of fun and play. It is well known in the American culture that competition is present all around us - many people believe it to be a natural way of existence. If this is true, how can we be competitive and "nice" to each other at the same time? Is it possible? Of course it is! I once read, and agree to the principle that, "Without a competitor, there is no competition" (in some circles this is a key objective). I interpret this to mean, "If nobody wants to play with you how much fun are you going to have?" What's my Point? Let's find a way to interact with a sense of COOPETITION – competing with each other while supporting efforts and actions, encouraging each other to do our best at any given time.

This is where ETIQUETTE PLAY comes in. Etiquette, simply put, means "good manners." Whenever I introduce the games in this book, I ask the players to use good manners – play with style. We often spend some time in a little discussion around what good manners looks like, but in all cases players walk away having experienced fun, excitement, and camaraderie among their competitors. Simply put, have fun and allow others to do the same. This is Etiquette Play.

Please, do not get me wrong here. I don't mean to convey the message that you should just go out and play these games being nicey-nicey to everyone and just let things go, play halfheartedly, and walk away without breaking a sweat. Each game should be played with a spirit of ADVENTURESOMENESS (what a great word – I found it in a game book from the 50s [I didn't say I found it in the 50s!]). The philosophy of Adventuresomeness is always choosing to take chances and play the game to the limits [and today I would add "safely"]. Play the game the way it is meant to be played – giving all you have with all you've got. You can surely go into a game of oveR the line and find it the most boring game you have ever played. However, if everyone is putting their energy into the serves and making

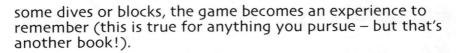

some dives or blocks, the game becomes an experience to remember (this is true for anything you pursue – but that's another book!).

Before you start any game, I encourage you to gather together and agree to interact within the spirit of ETIQUETTE PLAY, keep a mind-set of COOPETITION, and by all means give it all the ADVENTURESOMENESS you've got! Have fun and watch out, because here we go...........

sol-R (pronounced soul-are)

Applications: Sol-R is a great game for players to develop hand-eye coordination at their own speed. Players also learn to challenge themselves and establish personal bests. Sol-R can be played on small or large Spans, however, too many Sol-R games going at the same time, in the same area, can be hazardous.

Needs: 1 Ricochet' Ball and a ground level Span. (Playing this game on a table-top is really tough!) Remember to stretch out before playing!!

Number of Players: 1 (Do you get where I got sol-R from? If not, you can call me!)

Play: This game is a great way to get started and do some practicing on your own. Although there really is no way (at least we haven't done a formal study on it yet) to determine the reaction of the ball, you CAN work on your moves and reaction time.

In this game you will be the Thrower as well as the Receiver. If you want, just for practice, you can call the Throw to yourself, (but don't let anyone catch you talking to yourself, they may never want to play the games with you) – remember, either a Sneaker, a Skyscraper, or a Rocket (check the Lingo out if you have become confused). You get 10 Throws and 10 chances to catch for Points during this game. See how many Points you can accumulate after 10 Throws.

Scenario: Okay, let's go with a Skyscraper. You make the underhand Throw into the air. Let it hit the Span once, twice, three time – you'd better grab it!! YES! Nice Catch. You have 3 Points on the board. Let's stay with the Skyscraper one more time. Nice Throw, OH NO, Ricochet'. It's heading for the fence. Done Ball! No Points for that Throw. You still have 3 Points though (you never lose what you got!). Let's play it safe. Go for the Sneaker. Good, one, two, grab it! Okay, maybe a little too safe! But, you got two more. Total of 5 now, in three Throws. You've got seven more Throws left. Give it all you've got! What can you get?

Note: As far as I know to date, the sol-R record is 52 on a tennis court Span – outdoors I think.

Ideas, Records & Places:

_____

_____

_____

_____

_____

_____

_____

_____

_____

_____

_____

_____

Ideas, Records & Places:

_____

_____

_____

_____

_____

_____

_____

_____

_____

_____

_____

_____

_____

_____

_____

_____

_____

_____

_____

Ricochet'

Applications: Ricochet' is meant to be a competitive game, however, it tends to be so fun to watch that the spirit of Coopetition is easily attained. Players learn to accommodate each other to make the game play more smoothly, and learn how and when to take chances – to catch or not to catch. Players also partake in the roll of watching out for each other.

Ricochet' can be played on a variety of Spans from sidewalks to playgrounds. Each group of players will need a good deal of room for the game to play out well, however. So, several games going on at the same time will need a good deal of space. For a picture, one half of a tennis court works out great for one game. Keep the net up and you can play two games using one court. Every once in a while a stray ball may end up in the wrong court, but it really doesn't disrupt anything.

Needs: 1 Ricochet' ball. A ground level Span is best for this game – the larger the Span the more Points possible for each Throw.

Number of players: 2 to 6 is best – you could sneak in a couple more if the attention Span is good.

Play & Scenario in one: Gather the players on the Span and circle up. Number off the players from 1 to how ever many. If you are not into using the number 1 (for whatever reason), start with the number 6. This order will be the Throwing order for the game. Each player will be playing against all other players, but don't worry there will be some, "Coopetition" as well (see the "Lingo" pages).

The first thing you will need to do as a group is determine the Nature of Play you will follow during the game. I always encourage "Etiquette Play" whenever the Ricochet' ball is out (see, Etiquette Play section). However, there may be other natures for different groups. Whatever nature you choose, please take care of each other and all that is around you. So, propose a Nature of Play, make sure every player agrees – I like to use a thumbs-up around the circle – then before you get going, choose a Closing Score for the game. A game to 10 Points usually plays out pretty good. The player who reaches 10 (or above) and wins by two takes the game. (I have played games to 50+ Points because of the, "win by two" rule – you'll see.)

Here's how it plays. All the players stand around in a nice big circle. Each player has a fair amount of room to move around. For simplicity sake, let's say we have 4 players – numbers 1 through 4. The #1 players will Throw for the #2 player – called the Receiver. The #2 player will Throw for the #3 player (Receiver). The #3 player will Throw for the #4 player (Receiver). The #4 player Throws for the #1 player (Receiver). Let's start the game with # 1 Throwing. This player Throws for.................. that's right, #2 – you're sharp!

First, player #2 calls one of the three Throws – Sneaker, Skyscraper, or a Rocket (see, Lingo if you're lost). The Thrower will honor this call to the best of his or her ability (Coopetition) trying to "aim" the Throw so it strikes the Span close to the center of the circle of players – the center of the chosen Span. The Action-Time begins once the ball is Thrown in the air. Now, if you remember from the Lingo section, the Receiver (#2 player at this point) can call a Re-Throw before the ball touches the Span for the first time if the Receiver feels the Throw will put him or her at a disadvantage. The Re-Throw call stops the Action-Time. Any player can then Fetch the ball and Hand it back (don't Toss it back) to the Thrower for another Throw.

Let's regroup. The #1 player Throws for #2. The Throw is made, Action-Time begins. During Action-Time, the Receiver will be tracking the ball waiting for the opportunity to catch it. Each time the ball touches the Span it is counted for a Point. The Receiver can Catch the ball at any time he or she chooses to gain the Points counted. So, if the Receiver let the ball touch the Span three times and then caught it, he or she would gain three Points. These Points are never lost during the game. After the Catch, a Done-Ball is called and the Action-Time is over and Down-Time begins

During Action-Time, all the other players are making their best effort to stay out of the way of the Receiver. If any player gets in the way of the Receiver's attempt to track or Catch the ball, it is considered a Hinder and the Receiver gets another Throw. A Hinder is also called if any other player, other than the Receiver, touches the ball during Action-Time. Also, during Action-Time, all other players (not Receiving) are responsible for protecting the Receiver from running into any dangerous objects. Using the word WALL, in a loud voice, as a warning to the Receiver works out well. The Receiver then has the choice to heed the warning or not. There is one other important responsibility of the Non-Receiving Players during Action-Time. They will help to count the number of Points the ball makes and help to determine a good Catch, a Done-Ball, a Dud, a

Roller/Dribbler, and Touches (see, Lingo section). Non-Receivers are the Coopetitive judges of the game. Fair play is always recommended.

Now that player #2 has three Points, he is ready to be the Thrower for player #3. The Throw is made (after player #3 calls a specific Throw) and player #3 tracks the ball around the Span, he makes a try for the ball after 5 Points, but it bounces out of his hands and then hits the Span again. This is considered a Touch (called by the Receiver himself, or the Non-Receiving Players), and a Done-Ball. No Points are awarded to player #3. Player #3 Throws for player #4. Player #4 Catches after two Points and then Throws for player #1. After the Throw from player #4, the ball takes a mean Ricochet' and turns into a Rabbit that turns into a Roller. A Done-Ball is called for player #1 – no Points.

The first Round is over. Go around the circle and check Points - #1, 0 Points, #2, 3 Points, #3, 0 Points, #4, 2 Points. Move into Round two. Players keep their Points after each round and add to them after each turn – remember, players never lose Points.

Okay, we've played several Rounds and player #4 has a total of 11 Points. From this place in the game, each player (#1, #2 & #3) now has one Receiving attempt to get within 2 Points (a score of 10), tie the leader, or surpass the leader. (This gets a bit confusing, but hang in there, we're almost ready!)

Without going into a great big scenario, just think about this. Once there is a leader with 10 Points or more that is 2 Points ahead of all the other players, all the other players have one more chance to catch up to the leader to keep the game going. So, if another player in the game above makes it to 10 Points, the game continues around the circle. Player #4 gets another Throw for more possible Points. You can see how the game can last a long time.

So, there you have it? It seems quite complicated on paper, but once you play it a few times it makes more sense. If you have questions, please feel free to contact me!

Note: I have played this game all over the country. I've tried to explain the game to potential players, but failed to relate the intrigue of the game. Now I just get them on a Span and play. I have never seen a player walk off after a game who wasn't hooked for life. Why? I have been told it is fun because it has risk – when do I catch it? It is fun to watch. Inactive players are still responsible for parts of the game. It's competitive, but it doesn't seem like it. Winning doesn't seem that important because it's really not about skill, it's more about the "bounce" of the ball. And what is the bounce of the ball but a moment of chaos in the web of time that lasts only as long as it seems! Sorry, I get carried away.

The bottom line – make it work for you and please make it FUN!

Ideas, Records & Places:

_____

_____

_____

_____

_____

_____

_____

_____

_____

Ideas, Records & Places:

_____

_____

_____

_____

_____

_____

_____

_____

_____

_____

_____

_____

_____

_____

_____

_____

_____

_____

_____

_____

Ricochet' doubles

Applications: doubles Ricochet' (just like Ricochet') is meant to be a competitive game, but again, it tends to be so fun to watch that the spirit of Coopetition is easily attained. Players learn to accommodate each other to make the game play more smoothly, and learn how and when to

take chances – to catch or not to catch. An added facet to this variation is the teamwork component within each pair of players. Pairs of players have to learn to communicate with each other to become more successful at the task. Again, all players are asked to watch out for each other.

In doubles Ricochet' each 2 to 4 pairs of players will need a good deal of room for the game to play out well. So, several games going on at the same time will need a good deal of space. As in Ricochet', half of a tennis court works out great for one game. Keep the net up and you can play two games using one court.

Needs: 1 Ricochet' ball for groups of 2 to 4 pairs of players. A ground level Span with lots of room is best for this game.

Number of players: Doubles is played with 2 player teams. You'll need at least two teams of 2 players each – 4 players. A good maximum number is four small teams – 8 players. However, I have played games with six small teams – 12 players. So, what am I saying here!? You decide, but, you do need at least two teams of 2 players on each team!

Play: First, please read the directions for, Ricochet'. Doubles plays out the same basic way with some added excitement.

Done with that? Great! Now, here's the added fun. Choose a Throwing and Receiving order by teams. In Doubles, a team Throws to another team – it doesn't matter which player on the team Throws (most teammates will take turns as each round rolls around). As the Receiving team, it doesn't matter which player is the Receiver. Here's where it gets interesting.

Once the Throw is called and then made by the Throwing team, the Receiving team players move around the Points (bounces) of the R-Ball. A couple of things can happen. Either of the two Receiving players can Catch the ball for Points – the team takes those Points. Or, one of the Receiving players can initiate a "Push." A Push is done on the R-Ball as it is moving towards the Span. The Receiving players will track the ball and watch for the downward motion. If either player feels able to make a Push, he or she will call, "PUSH" to warn the other players of the impending action. Then, almost catching the ball, Push it, with some energy, into the Span to add more bounce (Points), and Action-Time, to the R-Ball. After the Push has been initiated, the player who Pushed the ball is no longer allowed to Catch it. His or her teammate must Catch the ball to gain the Points scored. Only one Push is allowed per turn.

The idea behind the Push is to extend the Action-Time on the R-Ball so a team can accumulate more Points. Since more Points can be achieved in a shorter time, a good Closing Score for a game of doubles is 20 Points.

The Non-Receiving Players have all the same responsibilities as in Ricochet'. They will also be monitoring the Push action. Remember, the R-Ball must be moving down towards the Span when a Push is made. If the ball is Pushed while moving away from the Span, a Touch is called.

Note: The action on the R-Ball after a Push is often erratic – even more than usual. So, making the call, "PUSH" is very important. After the warning, the player Pushing the ball should try to turn all vital body parts away from the bounce of the ball. All other players should also position themselves far enough away from the Push to ensure proper safety. (I always recommend a "side type" stance, in relation to the ball, at all times.) The bottom line – be extra mindful of the ball after a Push!

Ideas, Records & Places:

_____

_____

_____

_____

_____

_____

_____

Ideas, Records & Places:

_____

_____

_____

_____

_____

_____

_____

_____

_____

_____

_____

_____

_____

_____

_____

_____

_____

_____

_____

bReak out

Application: bReak out is a great cooperative game for small groups. Players have a chance to work on communication, hand-eye coordination, and empathy – everyone finds out real fast that it's not easy to catch that crazy ball. Players and groups as a whole, build together an exciting atmosphere as they learn to motivate each other to try and "beat that record." Several games of bReak out can be played at the same time in a gym or playground area since the Ricochet' balls are mainly contained within the group circles. Every once in a while a ball gets loose, but does not often find its way inside another circle of players.

Needs: 1 Ricochet' Ball. A small size Span will do - tabletops work great as well. Players will not have to run around during this game - unless they need to Fetch the ball. You will want enough room around the Span so players have about an arms length of room between them. If you are not using a table, you will also need some sort of boundary marking where Points will be scored. If you are outside you could make a big chalk circle. If you are inside you could use a big rope or masking tape. If in a basketball gym, the center circle or the circles around some free-throw areas

work out great.

Number of Players: 4 to 10 Players work well.

Play: Establish what the group will use as a Point boundary – circle, square, tabletop. Have the group stand around the outside of the boundary – as I mentioned before, arms length spacing makes a good challenge.

Here's how it plays. The ball will be Thrown, using Sneaker Throws, into the Point boundary area. Each time the ball hits this area on the Span the group gets a Point. Anyone can Catch the ball if it comes to him or her, however, no Player may enter the Point boundary area unless the ball has come to rest there. Once a Player Catches the ball he or she immediately makes a Sneaker Throw back into the middle of the Point boundary area. Our objective, as a group, is to gain as many Points as we can before the ball, "Brakes Out" of our circle (or square) of Players. This is where a clear boundary line comes in handy. If the ball hits the Span outside of the established boundary area, that round is over.

Once the group establishes a benchmark, see if they can beat it for a new world record.

Scenario: Six Players are standing poised and ready around the outside of the jump circle on a basketball court. John Throws up (not that "Throw Up") a good Sneaker, 1, 2, 3, Points – over to Mary - good Catch. Mary puts it right back into play. Another nice Sneaker, 4, 5, low trajectory over to Peter. GREAT Catch Pete! Pete Throws it back into play, 6, 7, 8, 9, 10, (staying in well), Dibble, Done-Ball. Susan steps into the boundary area to pick up the ball. Sue Throws it in, 11, 12, ohhhh, a sharp Ricochet' brakes out of the circle of Players and hits the floor outside the Point boundary. So, the group record is 10 Points – the last Catch they made. No, problem to break that record. We're just getting warmed up! Let's stay on our toes and back each other up – LET'S DO IT!!

Note: I like this game because it stresses the point about, "being there" and doing your part. We may not get the ball very much, or ever. But, if we weren't there how would that affect the team. Sometimes to make this point, I ask one or two of the players to just stand there and not attempt to Catch the ball. How will the other players react? What will they have to do?

Ideas, Records & Places:

_____

_____

_____

_____

_____

_____

_____

_____

_____

_____

_____

_____

_____

_____

Ideas, Records & Places:

_____

_____

_____

_____

_____

_____

_____

_____

_____

_____

_____

_____

_____

_____

_____

_____

_____

_____

_____

coopeRative Ricochet'

Application: In coopeRative Ricochet' players are given an opportunity to look at goal setting and how it works for individuals as well as how our goals can affect the group as a whole. Players are encouraged to assist the group in whatever way they can – however many Points they can get. They learn how to support each other and even understand how it is sometimes necessary to "do a little extra" for our teammates.

A group of 8 players will need a good amount of space for

this one – the size of a half a tennis court works well. If several groups are playing at the same time, it is best to have some sort of barrier between them.

Needs: 1 Ricochet' Ball. Any size Span will do – even a tabletop works well for this game.

Number of Players: 6 to 8 players work the best for this one. I've played with 10 before, there's just a bit more waiting around.

Play: The players will need to understand the basic premise of the Ricochet' game and the Lingo to understand this brief description. If you haven't done so yet, please read the

✳ ────────────────────────────── ✳

Ricochet' game description. You do not have to play Ricochet' to learn this one, you'll just need the concepts.

If I haven't played Ricochet' with my newly acquired R-Ball playing friends, I'll toss the ball around for a while so everyone can get used to how it bounces. Challenge the group to let it bounce as long as they can before Catching it.

With the R-Ball dynamics in mind, explain that each person in the group will make one Throw and Receive one Throw for the game, but first, as a group, we need to set a goal for ourselves. Go around the circle of players and ask, "How many Points will you make for this group?" (Translation: How many times do you think you can let the ball bounce before you Catch it?) Go around and total up all the individual "goals" to make a "group goal" for the first game. In most cases that I have seen, Players make pretty high goals to impress (or whatever) the other players. So, a group of 6 Players might end up with a group goal of 52, or something like that. Do not discourage high goal setting. Let the game go on.

Now that the group goal is set, find out who would like to start as the first Receiver. Review the Throws that are available and any other Lingo you will need to play this game out (see, Lingo section). Before starting, ask the group (or let them know) about the three levels of goal outcome. Does anyone know? You can meet your goal. You can come up short of your goal. And, you can exceed your goal. Although the Receiver has set a goal, it will be up to that person to choose when the best time to Catch the ball will be. Herein lies the RISK! Gotta love it!

Scenario: Let's use a simple example. We have 6 Players, all choosing to Catch the ball after 5 bounces (Points) for a group goal of 30 Points. The first Receiver asks and gets a Skyscraper. Good bounces, he Catches it after 5. The group is on track. The next Player asks for a Sneaker. Ohhh, bad luck, the ball Rabbits out and into the fence, Done-Ball. Okay, we're at 50% of our goal. We can make it up!? The next four Players are able to Catch some Points but the group could not make its 30 Points. Now what? Let's play again. Now that we have some more information about the dynamics of the game, let's set another group goal and try again.

Note: The idea behind this game is about goal setting (but you knew that!). The first game tends to be high, the second game tends to be low. Then, as the Players get comfortable, they can start making the game a challenge with exciting conclusions. I have seen some great strategies around the Throw Receiving order, going, "over budget" to meet the goal, bringing in more help to reach the goal, and so on. Also, be very aware of the language used during the game. Supportive communication is the only language I allow. Without support, it is very difficult to reach our goals. And besides, the "random" action of the ball misleads us at times (seeing any "metaphors" here?). Bottom line as always, have FUN and stop while the energy is good so the group will want to play again at another time.

Ideas, Records & Places:

_____

_____

_____

_____

_____

_____

_____

_____

_____

_____

Ideas, Records & Places:

_____

_____

_____

_____

_____

_____

_____

_____

_____

_____

_____

_____

_____

_____

_____

_____

_____

oveR the line

Applications: If played with that Adventuresomeness, oveR the line is just darn exciting. It heightens hand-eye coordination (in fact, it is a pre-requisite for safe play) and body awareness. Games of oveR the line are fast paced and energetic, and often addicting – a positive addiction.

Every 10 players will need about a 30 x 30 foot area to play and it is a great benefit to have some sort of barriers behind each team – or someone is going to have to do lots of Fetching (however, the aerobic benefits are advantageous). This is one of those games that does have the potential for "busted lips" (as my friend says). So, bear this in mind when deciding who might want to play, and who will have the needed skills to keep themselves from getting "busted" as we say.

Needs: 1 Ricochet' Ball. The optimal Span is the backcourt of a tennis court with doubles lines marked out – 18 feet

wide by 27 feet long. However, you can set up your own Span for play. You will need two lines facing each other 27 feet apart. You can draw the lines with chalk, use masking tape, or set out two cones and set the "invisible" line between them (the invisible line is harder to use when calling the close ones – it's really best to have a visible line of some sort). The width will depend on the number of players you have. I have played with 2 to 5 players on a team – you need two teams. A challenging width is about five feet of line for each player. So, let's say you have four players. Set up your lines 27 feet apart and 20 feet wide. If you have a cone for each end of your lines, all the better. If you don't, no problem. (Check out the court set-up in the diagram provided.)

Number of Players: Two teams of equal number from 2 to 5 players on a team. (If there are extra players, I like to rotate players in. These players make great referees while waiting to rotate in.)

Suggested Age: 13 and older

Play: oveR the line is a variation of the old time favorite battle game of Guts played with a Frisbee (or other flying disc). Two lines face off against each other to blast the disc through the lines. For, oveR the line, I want to take a little bit of the "blast" out of it, but keep the fun! Stick with me on the explanation. It's going to be wordy, but the payoff is a great game!

The objective in oveR the line is for each team to score points by getting the Ricochet' ball "over" the other teams playing line and then touching the ground in the "Scoring Zone" area (See court set-up diagram provided.). A good Closing Score is anywhere from 5 to 7 points – win by 2. (10 points gets a bit long at times.) OveR the line is meant to be a fast paced game, loaded with excitement – keep this in mind. The game can be played slowly, but what fun would that be?

Once the court is set up, players must be positioned

somewhere in their Scoring Zone area behind the Playing
Line for the serve. Let's give the ball to team "A" for the
serve. Any player on team "A" can make the serve. On the
serve:

1.   <u>The server must have both big toes on his or her
Playing Line, or just behind it.</u> If a server is standing over
the line or steps back behind the line too far, a NO SERVE is
called.

2.   <u>The ball must stay within the frontal plane of the
server's body during the serve.</u> (This is a bit hard to explain
on paper. I'll do my best.) If the server is toeing-the-line,
he or she has their shoulders parallel to the other team's
line (so to speak). Keeping this stance, the ball must remain
in front of the server's body at all times - in front of the
Playing Line. In other words, the server may not bring the
ball back behind his or her body at any time during the
serve. This is how I've taken out some of the "blast" to
make it a bit safer. So, the serve takes on more of a pushing
motion. I have seen some very creative serves from very
slow to fast – all from the frontal plain of the body. If the

ball is seen going behind the frontal plain, a NO SERVE is called. Bottom line – we don't want overhand fastballs here!! (See pictures on previous page.)

3.　　The ball must bounce at least once before it reaches the other teams playing line. If it doesn't bounce once, a NO SERVE is called.

Okay, back to the action. Team "A" makes a good serve. Now, team "B" plays the ball. To play the ball:

1.　　All players must stay behind their own playing line and wait for the serve to come to them. No player from either team is allowed in the front field area (see diagram) before the serve reaches the playing line of the Receiving Team.

2.　　Players may catch the ball when it comes to them. After a Catch, the ball can be served right up.

3.　　Players may also "Block" the ball when it comes to them. A couple things can happen after a block. The ball may go up and behind the line - Any player on team "B" can catch this ball. (If the ball comes down to touch the Scoring Zone, a point goes to team "A.") Also, the ball could be blocked into the field – either the front-field or back-field. (See diagram.) This is a "free" ball. Any player on either team can go to get the ball in either field. This as called a, "Field-R" (fielder). Most often, opposing players will come out for a Field-R if the ball goes into the front-field. Less often for back-field balls – but back-field balls are free balls after the ball is touched. (More on Field-Rs in a moment.)

Once team "B" has possession of the ball, they become the servers, following serving rules.

If the ball happens to come down and touch the Scoring Zone, team "A" gets a Point. The team "B" server then Toes-The-Line for the next serve.

Let's go back to the Field-R. This is where the excitement

abounds. If the ball is blocked out into the front-field, any number of players can go after it. (I allow for a little body contact here, but I keep it fun at all cost.) Now, keep in mind, if players go out into the field it will leave "holes" at the Playing Lines. Let's say 2 players from each team of 5 players come out into the front-field for the ball. A player from team "A" scoops up the ball. From here he can run back to the playing line and serve it up or (more often than not) he can toss it back to one of his teammates, who is behind the playing line for that team. This player can serve it right up – following the serving rules. Now, on this serve from team "A" several things can happen:

1.   If the ball hits a player in the front-field from team "A" the ball is called a Done-Ball – play stops - and team "B" gets the serve.

2.   If the ball hits a player in the front-field from team "B", <u>after a bounce,</u> team "A" scores a point – team "B" gets the serve. If the ball hits a team "B" player on the fly, it is a Done-Ball – play stops - and team "B" gets the serve.

3.   Team "A" can serve the ball towards an open hole in the line where it might be caught by a team "B" player or sneak through for a score.

In any case, the players that go out into the field will want to get out of the way as soon as possible once the ball is scooped up and passed to a Serving Player. The fastest way out is off to the sides.

Something else might happen as well. The team "A" player in the front-field tosses the ball back to his line, but his teammate drops the ball and it touches within the scoring zone! Point for team "B." Any time the ball touches the scoring zone, after a serve or pass back, is a point for the opposing team. Only 1 Point can be scored per serve or pass back drop. Multiple bounces in the scoring zone are not multiple Points.

Okay, now you have the ground rules. Here are a couple

other items to keep in mind:

When setting up the Scoring Zone, make sure each team has the same size zone. There is no out-of-bounds, only a front-field, back-field, and a scoring zone. Remember, any player can go after a ball when it's in one of the fields after being touched by a player from the Receiving Team.

Scenario: Okay, with the rules at hand, let's talk some play. There are 4 players on each team – "A" & "B". "Allen" serves the ball. It gets one good bounce before "Bobby" catches it. Since Bobby is over at one end of the Playing Line, he hands it over to Betty. She serves it up – a nice high looper over to team "A". The ball bounces over team "As" playing line, but Ashley backs up to make the catch. Ashley Toes-The-Line and sends out a Rocket serve. After one low bounce the ball breaks through and touches the Scoring Zone – point for team "A". Bobby Fetches up the ball and Hands it to Bill for the serve. A low ball with several bounces. Allen blocks the ball into the front-field. Two players from each team run out to get the ball. Brandy manages to scoop up the ball and lobs it back to Betty. The players in the field move to the sides as Betty serves a fastball down the center. The ball takes a quick fade to the left, breaks through the line, and touches the Scoring Zone – Point for team "B". It's 1 to 1 with team "A" serving.

Keeping the game fast paced makes it a lot more fun. Also, keep in mind, there is a greater potential for balls in the face during this game. Be ever mindful of this happening. Quick reflexes are the key. I would avoid playing this game with younger players. Older players will have a little more "reflex" practice. To make this game a bit safer, you can always spread the Playing Lines out farther – 30 to 35 feet will give more reaction time on the ball.

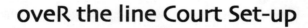

oveR the line Court Set-up

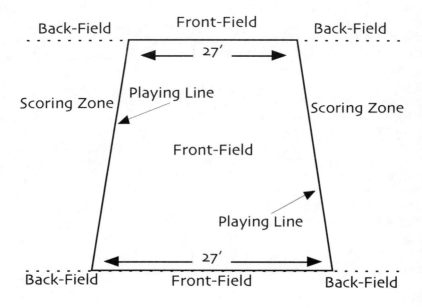

Ideas, Records & Places:

_____

_____

_____

_____

_____

_____

_____

_____

_____

_____

_____

_____

_____

_____

_____

_____

_____

_____

_____

Rocce Ball

Application: Rocce ball is intended as a fun interaction game between players. It's not so much the skill involved in the game (you can never get the ball where you want it to go), it's more about how you play the game and interact with each other. I have witnessed Bocce games (the cousin of Rocce) in distant lands where players just wander around town playing Bocce and socializing – tossing the target ball from place to place. It was hard to tell if they ever kept score, it seemed more about being together with friends and sharing some time together.

Rocce can be played on many open Spans with open Spaces or indoors, off the wall, by several groups at the same time if everyone has a Ricochet' ball. This one's about playing, socializing, and having some fun. I could see clusters of players roaming the streets with their Ricochet' balls, couldn't you?

Needs: Each player will need their own Ricochet' ball for this one – I find it helpful for each player to put their name on the ball or some sort of marking to identify each one. You'll need a target-ball of some kind as well – a tennis ball, a golf ball, or even another Ricochet' Ball. Also, any good size Span will do for this game. One of my favorites includes

46

a wall to play off – the wall version allows for groups to utilize smaller spaces indoors and out.

Number of Players: I have played this one with anywhere from 2 to 5 players per game. If I have more players than 6, I split them up into more teams playing separate games.

Suggested Age: 7 and older

Play: Rocce (rochee) is a spin off of the international game of Bocce. Here's how it goes. One player is chosen to toss the target-ball out into the playing field. He can play the target-ball off a wall or toss it out into an open Span. Encourage short throws versus long ones. Short throws tend to keep the action a bit more even. Long throws tend to be very hard to measure.

So, after a nice toss out into the playing field each player takes a turn tossing his or her own Ricochet' ball towards the target-ball. If the target-ball was thrown off a wall, each player must also toss his or her Ricochet' Ball off the same wall. The player who manages to get his or her ball closest to the target-ball receives 3 points. The next closest ball to the target-ball gets 1 point (if there are only two players in the game, the closest Ricochet' Ball to the target-ball gets one point – play to 10 points). If there are any discrepancies about which ball is closer, use your spirit of Coopetition and find a solution. The one used most often is redoing the round.

The player who scores the highest in each round will be the target-ball thrower for the next round. Remember, discourage those long lobbing target-ball throws. For groups of 3 or more players, I usually have them play games up to 20 points – win by two. This seems to go quickly.

Note: Most groups find the "off-the-wall" version a bit more contained and more interesting to watch – all the throws and rolls are really close. Use whatever fits your group and whatever space you have.

Ideas, Records & Places:

_____

_____

_____

_____

_____

_____

_____

_____

_____

_____

_____

_____

_____

_____

_____

_____

_____

_____

_____

R v-ball

Applications: R v-ball is a great lead-up and variation to volleyball. Players work on communication skills, hand-eye coordination, and decision-making abilities. It is limited to a standard volleyball set-up or a rope strung between two upright standards, and a maximum of 12 players per game (6 per team).

Needs: You will need 1 or 2 Ricochet' balls for this one depending on which variation you use. The Span is a standard volleyball court (not sand volleyball) and set-up with a net. The normal court dimensions are 30' by 60' with the net splitting the court in half so each team has a 30' by 30' area to work in. The net (or rope) should be at least as high, or higher than the tallest player in the game. Don't worry, spiking will not be allowed.

Number of Players: Two teams of equal number from 2 to 6 players on a team. (If there are extra players, I like to rotate players in. These players make great referees while waiting to rotate in.)

Suggested Age: 10 and older

Play: Replace the standard volleyball with a Ricochet' ball and you have an interesting game. Here are the adaptations.

If you have less than 4 players per team you may choose to shorten the boundaries up a bit – however, it is not required for full action. The serve is made from the 10-foot line (10 feet from the net on the serving team's side). The service should be a nice lob over the net and land somewhere near the center of the 10-foot line on the opponent's side. If the ball looks as though it is going to be too off center, the Receiving Team can call a Re-Throw. The Receiving Team can let the ball bounce as many times as they would like before they attempt to Catch it for Points. Each bounce inside the Receiving Teams court (30' by 30' square) is worth one Point. Someone on the Receiving Team must catch the ball in order to obtain the Points for that serve. If the Ricochet' ball touches the Span outside of the Receiving Team's court, no Points are awarded. If the ball touches any of the Receiving Team players, without being caught, no points are awarded. However, if the ball caroms off a Receiving Team player and then a teammate catches the ball before it hits the ground, the team receives the Points for that service.

As you can tell from the adaptations, the serving team does not get any Points like in the traditional game of volleyball. Points are awarded to the Receiving Team after Catching the Ricochet' ball after it has hit the Span any number of times. A game to 25 Points keeps the excitement going.

An interesting variation of this game involves simultaneous serving. Each team serves to the other at the same time. I will usually introduce this as a warm-up before getting into the head-to-head (or heads-to-heads) Coopetition.

Note: Remember to inform the players to keep an eye out for each other. Volleyball poles do not render right-of-way. Put those "Wall" calls to use if needed.

Ideas, Records & Places:

_____

_____

_____

_____

_____

_____

_____

_____

_____

_____

_____

_____

_____

_____

_____

_____

_____

_____

Racks

Application: Like Rocce ball, Racks is intended as a fun solo game or an interactive game between players. It's not so much the skill involved in the game it's more about how you play the game and interact with each other. Racks is a grander, and a bit more crazy, form of Jacks which came from 5 stones – but that's another story. Players can develop some great hand-eye-to-hand coordination. Planning skills as well as decision making also play a part in this activity. Players will need a good amount of room for this one – about a 30 x 30 foot space is good. If there are other games of Racks around, it is best to have some sort of barrier between them.

Needs: 1 Ricochet' ball for every 1 to 4 players. You will also need 6 "wads" as well. Wads are larger objects like, balled-up newspaper tapped together with masking tape, empty gallon milk jugs (this version is fun to watch), or half inflated beach balls. As for the Span, a variety of ground level one's can work for this one.

Number of Players: Racks can be played solo, or in groups of up to 4 players – you can play with more, but there will be extended waiting around time. However, Racks is great fun to watch!

Suggested Age: 10 and older

Play: If you know how to play the traditional form of Jacks then you're ahead of the game a bit. I have a slight modification to speed up the process. Here's how I play it.

Gather up all 6 wads in your arms, holding them close to your chest. Stand up nice and tall, now "drop" the wads to the ground. (I would not recommend throwing the wads up into the air, the dispersal might be a bit tough to gather.)

There is a progression you will follow – Onesies, Twosies, Threesies, Foursies, Fivesies, and Sixies.

Onesies – Throw the Ricochet' ball into the air (now, the height of the Throw is up to you – as you read on you may be able to determine what you need). You will want to avoid hitting any wads with the descending Ricochet' ball, so make the proper Throw adjustments. Okay, back to the Throw. Make your Throw. Now, pick up one wad, hold onto it, wait for the Ricochet' ball to contact the Span one time, then Catch the ball. You must end up with both the wad and the ball in your possession for you to pass out of this level. If you are successful in this endeavor you have made it past onesies. Hand the ball to the next player. If you miss or drop the ball or the wad, Fetch the ball and Hand it to the next player. (If you're playing solo just try again.)

It will be up to you or the group whether a "drop" is done before each turn, or if players just return the wad(s) to where they picked them up.

Twosies – When the ball comes around to you again, and you have passed Onesies, Throw it up again (you know what I mean). Now, pick up two wads, wait for the ball to bounce off the Span one time, then Catch the ball. Whether you Catch the ball or not, it is always passed to the next player. You cannot move on to the next level until you have passed the preceding one.

Threesies – Throw and pick up 3 wads, then Catch the ball after one bounce.

Foursies – Throw and pick up 4 wads, then Catch the ball after one bounce. (Can you see in your mind's eye how much fun the milk jugs would be!?)

Fivesies – Throw and pick up 5 wads, then Catch the ball after one bounce.

Sixies – Throw and pick up 6 wads, then Catch the ball after one bounce. (I have met few players who were able to pick up 6 milk jugs and Catch the ball – but, I have seen it done.)

Those are the basics. If you want to set up the game where you give players more bounces, that works too. It's hard to say if this variation is easier, but some players will perceive it to be so.

How does it end? (What movie?) Well you could say the first person to pass Sixies might win – giving every player a shot to tie. You could play until everyone makes Sixies. You could play until dinner. You could all pick up a wad on the last throw and watch the ball bounce around till it's Done. Or, just end your way. But what is my way? (What movie?

– same one as above.)

If you know Jacks, then you know there are some different challenges as well. One of the challenges I have tried is "wads in the basket." This one works well with younger players who don't have the wing-Span to hold all the wads. You'll need a good size basket – one that will (just) fit all the wads. Go through the progression above, but instead of holding the wads in your arms, place them in the basket, and then Catch the ball.

Partner Racks: This is a fun variation for pairs of players. Go through the progression above, but throw the wads to your partner, then, Catch the ball. The partner who caught the first wad is the next thrower when the ball comes around again. The first Thrower now has to catch two wads. Continue the process all the way to Sixies (You're getting that "milk jug" picture in your head aren't you?).

Ideas, Records & Places:

_____

_____

_____

_____

_____

_____

_____

_____

_____

_____

one moRe

Applications: one moRe is set up as a group challenge. Players work together to "beat the balls" (careful!). Strategies, creative planning, and problem solving are all a part of one moRe. Also, if you're working on theories of random chaos, this is the game for you.

Several games of one moRe can be played near each other. The Ricochet' balls are usually quite contained – but you know, as soon as I say that!!

Needs: I have not seen more than 6 Ricochet' balls Caught at the same time, but if you're up for it? Have at least 6 R balls on hand – more if you dare.

Number of Players: A good number for a 6 attempt is 8 players. However, lower the number of players, you raise the challenge of the game.

Suggested Age: 10 and older

Play: Gather the group around in a loose circle. Throw one Ricochet' ball up. The height of the Throws will be up to the group – part of the problem solving. Let the ball hit the

56

Span once, then someone in the group needs to catch it
before it hits the Span again. Now, my friend Mike Spiller
says that this could just be luck. So, take another Throw
with one ball, let it hit, then Catch it. When one ball is
Caught twice in a row, the group can move on to two
Ricochet' balls.

The group has to make two Catches in a row at each level to
be able to add "one moRe."

Throw two Ricochet' balls into the air at the same time.
After they both hit the Span the R-Balls must be Caught
before hitting the Span again. Now, Catching two balls
does not mean you Caught them twice in a row. Throw the
two Ricochet' balls in the air again and Catch them both
after each takes a bounce. If the group can Catch both twice
in a row, add one moRe.

Progress up as many levels as you can as a group. Be aware
that it does get a bit chaotic "in there." (You'll see.) It will
be very important for your group to have a plan-of-action
so-as-to avoid head-on contact.

When to stop? I think there's a game still going! Have
Fun!

Ideas, Records & Places:

_____

_____

_____

_____

_____

_____

_____

_____

_____

_____

_____

_____

_____

_____

_____

_____

_____

_____

_____

_____

_____

✣ ———————————————————— ✣

About the Author

CHRIS CAVERT has been active with groups of all ages for over 20 years. He has been a Camp Counselor, Classroom Instructor, Program Director for the YMCA, and a Classroom

Teacher. Chris has been the Director for two Challenge Course Adventure Programs and has lead backcountry trips all over the United States. He holds a Bachelors degree in Physical Education and a Masters Degree in Experiential Education specializing in curriculum development. To date, Chris is the author of six books and the co-author of two more. Chris primarily focuses on developing and sharing activities that help educators, in many different fields, use experiential education to encourage pro-social community building behaviors in the groups that they work with.

At the present time, Chris is the owner of FUNdoing, an Educational Activities Training Program provider. He leads Workshops and Trainings all over the country bringing the activities in his books to life. Chris works with and trains

Educators, Counselors, Recreational Staff, Camp Staff, Youth Workers, and Challenge Course Facilitators from coast to coast.

For more information about Chris' Books and Training Programs, visit:

www.fundoing.com

You will find:
* available workshops and trainings here and there,
* information for each book,
* more activities each week,
* more Ricochet' ball activities and information,
* links to other FUN sites,
* more fun products, Ricochet' balls, the PVCystem, and
* other fun people.

Books by Chris Cavert, (a.k.a., FUNdoing)

Purchase the following books through, Wood N Barnes
Publishing at, 1-800-678-0621

❋ E.A.G.E.R. Curriculum: Experiential Activities, Games, and Educational Recreation.
(11 chapters of activities from icebreakers to problem
solving elements, summer weather activities to crafts. A
great resource for schools, camps, residential facilities, and
recreation programs.)

❋ Games (and other stuff) for Group, Books I & II.
(Two books full of 5 to 10 minute activities that can be used
in small group settings to initiate conversations about a
variety of subjects. A great resource for counselors,
teachers, and youth workers.)

❋ Affordable Portables: A Working Book of Initiative Activities & Problem Solving Elements.
(Loads of portable activities you can make and use to start
or enhance any adventure programming.)

❋ Games (and other stuff) for Teachers: Classroom Activities that Promote Pro-Social Learning.
w/Laurie Frank. (Activities that can be done in a traditional
classroom setting that develop pro-social skills/behaviors.)

❋ What Would It Be Like?: 1,001 Anytime Questions for Anysize Answers.
(Loads of questions that start with, What would it be
like.... that can be used by counselors, teachers, youth
workers, or just about anyone interested in sharing
personal experiences and perspectives on a wide range of
topics. A great resource for discussion groups.)

The following books can be purchased through
Learning Unlimited Corporation:
www.learningunlimited.com
1-888-622-4203

✽ 50 Ways to Use Your Noodle: Loads of Land Games with Foam Noodle Toys.

w/Sam Sikes. (30 games and 20 problem solving activities using those foam noodle pool toys. Great for camps, schools, recreation, and adventure programming.)

✽ Ricochet' and Other Games with an Odd Ball.

(10 active group games, both competitive and cooperative types, using a unique 6-bump ball.)

Let Chris show you how to use all the great activities in his books.

COMING SOON!

50 More Ways To Use Your Noodle: More Games And Fun With Foam Noodle Toys
by Chris Cavert & Sam Sikes

Teambuilding Hardware
by Jim Cain, Chris Cavert & Sam Sikes

Contact Chris by
Voice at: 1-888-638-6565 or
E-mail: chris@fundoing.com

Notes:

Notes:

Notes:

Notes: